I CAN BE A

MUSICIAN

By Rebecca Hankin

Prepared under the direction of Robert Hillerich, Ph.D.

 CHILDRENS PRESS ™

CHICAGO

Library of Congress Cataloging in Publication Data

Hankin, Rebecca.
  I can be a musician.

  Summary: Describes different kinds of work
musicians can do.
  1. Music—Juvenile literature. [1. Music—
Vocational guidance] I. Title. II. Title: Musician
ML3928.H3 1984   780'.23   84-12136
ISBN 0-516-01844-2

PICTURE DICTIONARY

drum · tuba · trombone · trumpet · flute

marching band

conductor

orchestra

studio

guitar

band

musician

practice

lesson

piano

radio

record

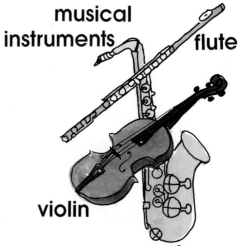

musical
instruments

flute

violin

saxophone

Saxophone

Clarinet

Music—it's everywhere!
We hear it on the radio
and TV. We hear it on
records. We can even go
to special places to
hear music.

radio

record

Guitar

Violin

Flute

Musicians are special people. They play the music we hear.

musician

There are many different kinds of musicians. Some musicians sing. Others play the piano or violin. Still others play the flute, guitar, or saxophone.

piano

flute

violin

saxophone

Rock band

There are many different musical instruments. Musicians use them to make music.

Some musicians work together in a small group called a band. Some bands have guitars, drums, and singers. People like to listen to band music.

band

Marching band

This band has more instruments. It has trumpets, trombones, flutes, tubas, and drums. This is a marching band.

marching band

Orchestra with singers

Sometimes musicians work together in a large group. It is called an orchestra. An orchestra has many different musical instruments.

orchestra

Conductor

A special person
called a conductor leads
the orchestra. The
musicians watch the
conductor as they play
their music. People enjoy
hearing the music. They
like watching the
conductor and the
musicians make their
music.

conductor

Banjo

Some musicians make music by themselves.

This girl sings and plays the banjo. Her friends and family like to hear her music.

Guitar

Sometimes musicians make records. They go to a special place called a studio.

studio

This singer is making a record of his songs. The studio musicians help the singer. They play their musical instruments while the singer sings.

These students are learning to play recorders in school.

Some good musicians become music teachers. They help students become good musicians too.

Trumpet

Bass fiddle

Piano

To be good, all musicians must practice. Practice is the way musicians learn to play well. The music must be played again and again. Musicians practice until they think their music sounds good.

practice

Practice is hard work. But a good musician knows that hard work is important.

This teacher gives piano lessons.

This boy takes piano lessons every week. His piano teacher helps him learn the music he plays. He must practice every day to play the music well. With hard work, this boy may become a very good musician.

lesson

Harp

French horn

It takes many years to become a musician. Some musicians study music at college. Others do not. But all musicians must work hard to become good at what they do.

Music is a very special thing. It brings happiness to people who listen to it. It also brings happiness to musicians who make it. Would you like to be a musician?

WORDS YOU SHOULD KNOW

band (BAND)—a group of musicians who play together

college (KAHL • ij)—a school for higher learning. It follows high school.

conductor (kuhn • DUHK • ter)—a person who leads a group such as a band or orchestra

drum (druhm)—a musical instrument that has a skin stretched across an opening. The player beats on the skin to make sounds.

drummer (DRUHM • er)—a person who plays a drum

enjoy (en • JOI)—to be happy with something

everywhere (ev • REE • [h]ware)—in all places or in each part or place

flute (FLOOT)—a long, thin musical instrument that is played by blowing across a hole near one end.

guitar (gi • TAHR)—a musical instrument with a flat body, a long neck, and usually six strings. The strings are pulled with the fingers or with a pick.

instrument (IN • struh • ment)—a thing that is used. Instruments are used to make music.

lesson (LES • un)—something that is to be studied and learned

musical (MYOO • zi • kuhl)—having to do with music

musician (myoo • ZISH • uhn)—a person who makes up, plays, or leads music

orchestra (OR • kes • truh)—a group of musicians who play together.

piano (pee • AN • oh)—a large musical instrument with wire strings and, usually, eighty-eight keys.

record (REK • erd)—a kind of thin, flat, round plate that has sound on it and that can be played on a record player.

singer (SING • er)—one who sings

studio (STOO • dee • oh)—a special place where records and TV or radio shows are made

study (STUHD • ee)—to try to learn by reading and thinking

trombone (trahm • BOHN or TRAHM • bohn)—a brass wind instrument with a long, thin tube with two turns in it. The tube ends in a bell shape.

trumpet (TRUHM • pit)—a brass wind instrument made of a thin, rounded tube that ends in a bell shape.

tuba (TOO • buh)—a large brass wind instrument that makes very deep sounds

violin (vy • uh • LIN)—a musical instrument with a flat body, a long neck, and four strings.

INDEX

band, 9, 11

banjo, 17

college, 27

conductor, 15

drums, 9, 11

flute, 7, 11

guitar, 7, 9

instruments, 11, 13

lessons, 25

marching band, 11

orchestra, 13

piano, 7, 25

practice, 23, 25

radio, 5

records, 5, 19

saxophone, 7

singer, 9

studio, 19

teachers, music, 21

trombones, 11

trumpet, 11

tubas, 11

TV, 5

violin, 7

PHOTO CREDITS

Nawrocki Stock Photo:
© Ken Sexton—4 (top left), 5 (right), 6 (top right), 14
© Jim Wright—18
© Phylane Norman—4 (bottom)
© Mike Kidulich—6 (top left), 22 (top right)
© William S. Nawrocki—6 (bottom)
© Candee Productions—10
© J. Steere—Cover, 12
© Image Finders—5 (left)
© Jacqueline Durand—7, 26 (bottom)

Hillstrom Stock Photos:
© Milton and Joan Mann—20, 22 (bottom), 24, 29
© Laurel Spingola—8
© Don and Pat Valenti—16, 22 (top left)

Tom Stack & Associates:
© Sheryl S. McNee—26 (top)
© Liz Jaquith—28
© Don and Pat Valenti—4 (top right)

COVER: Rehearsal of Chicago Symphony Orchestra with the Glen Ellyn Children's Chorus

About the Author

Rebecca Hankin is a writer and editor who lives in Chicago.